BREAD MACHINE COOKBOOK FOR BEGINNERS

1000 Days of Quick and Easy Homemade Recipes to Get Your Fresh, Fragrant, and Tasty Bread Every Day without Effort

Amber Wexler

Table of Contents

Measurement Conversion Table

VOLUME EQUIVALENTS(DRY)

US STANDARD	METRIC (APPROXIMATE)
1/8 teaspoon	0.5 mL
1/4 teaspoon	1 mL
1/2 teaspoon	2 mL
3/4 teaspoon	4 mL
1 teaspoon	5 mL
1 tablespoon	15 mL
1/4 cup	59 mL
1/2 cup	118 mL
3/4 cup	177 mL
1 cup	235 mL
2 cups	475 mL
3 cups	700 mL
4 cups	1 L

WEIGHT EQUIVALENTS

US STANDARD	METRIC (APPROXIMATE)
1 ounce	28 g
2 ounces	57 g
5 ounces	142 g
10 ounces	284 g
15 ounces	425 g
16 ounces (1 pound)	455 g
1.5 pounds	680 g
2 pounds	907 g

VOLUME EQUIVALENTS(LIQUID)

US STANDARD	US STANDARD (OUNCES)	METRIC (APPROXIMATE)
2 tablespoons	1 fl.oz.	30 mL
1/4 cup	2 fl.oz.	60 mL
1/2 cup	4 fl.oz.	120 mL
1 cup	8 fl.oz.	240 mL
1 1/2 cup	12 fl.oz.	355 mL
2 cups or 1 pint	16 fl.oz.	475 mL
4 cups or 1 quart	32 fl.oz.	1 L
1 gallon	128 fl.oz.	4 L

TEMPERATURES EQUIVALENTS

FAHRENHEIT(F)	CELSIUS(C) (APPROXIMATE)
225 °F	107 °C
250 °F	120 °C
275 °F	135 °C
300 °F	150 °C
325 °F	160 °C
350 °F	180 °C
375 °F	190 °C
400 °F	205 °C
425 °F	220 °C
450 °F	235 °C
475 °F	245 °C
500 °F	260 °C

Introduction to the Use of the Bread Machine

What Can a Bread Machine Do?

Bread machines can differ in design, capacity, number of accessories, and available programs. When choosing a bread machine, think about your preferences and needs: What will you do with the machine? Do you need special programs and additional modes, or is the basic functionality sufficient?

Bread machines can knead, rest the dough, bake a crisp baguette, make sweet cupcakes or unleavened bread, and more.

When you get to know this handy device, it will truly become an essential and an exceptional aid in your kitchen.

It's so simple:

1. Insert the baking sheet into the machine
2. Attach the dough blades
3. Add ingredients, as shown in your machine manual
4. Close the lid
5. Turn on the machine
6. Select the required function

How to Use a Bread Machine

Equipment Needed

Because the bread machine is so wonderfully self-contained, you won't need much other equipment to get started on making fantastic bread. Most likely, your bread machine will include baking pans, but you will also need to ensure you have a good quality cooling rack for freshly baked bread: putting hot loaves on a flat surface can trap steam at the bottom of the bread, causing a soggy bottom. Since the one thing the bread machine does not do is slice bread, you will need to make sure you have a good, sharp bread knife. A bread knife has a wide serrated edge that makes it easy to cut the loaf and get perfectly even slices, no matter what kind of bread you are slicing.

Learning The Controls

Although bread machines vary slightly by brand, most have the following functions that allow you to make different types of bread:

Cycle button: This button allows you to choose the type of bread you want to prepare.

Choose from: basic, French, gluten-free, quick, sweet, dough, jam, and cake. Continue pressing the Select button to scroll through the options.

Crust Color button: The bread machine allows you to choose from three different crust colors: Light, Medium, and Dark. Continue pressing this button to scroll through the dark options.

Loaf Size: With this button, you can choose whether to make a 1.5-pound loaf or a 2-pound loaf. Display: The LCD display allows you to view the current baking settings. You can view the type of bread you are making and the color setting, as well as the remaining time of the baking cycle.

Delay time: if you want to prepare bread later, you can adjust the time until the bread machine starts kneading/baking.

Start/Stop: if you want to prepare bread immediately, pressing this key starts the baking process.

The Cooking Process

Since bread making is a complicated scientific process, it is important to understand what the bread machine does during the baking process. This will enable you to get perfect loaves of bread with every baking!

Mixing yeast: The process begins as soon as you add the yeast to the other ingredients. As the ingredients are combined, the yeast starts to release carbon dioxide, which allows the bread to rise and form bubbles.

Kneading: The bread machine bakes the bread and does the hard work of kneading the dough. Once the kneading is started, the bread machine will begin to combine all the ingredients evenly. To get evenly baked bread, the ingredients must be evenly incorporated. This step is also important for forming gluten, the protein that makes bread chewy and soft (if gluten-free ingredients are used, this step will not form gluten).

Rising: Once the kneading is finished, the bread machine lets the dough rise for an appropriate amount of time. During this time, the yeast will have a chance to create more bubbles, allowing the bread to reach the proper height when baked. Since it is difficult to know how long to let the dough rise, the bread machine is programmed to know exactly how long to rise to get a perfect loaf.

Baking: After the dough has had enough time to rise, the baking process is automatically started. The bread machine will bake the bread for the optimal amount of time, depending on the bread being made and individual preferences.

Bread Machine Cycles and Techniques

Bread machines are a fantastic kitchen accessory.

These compact little wonders have many options and settings for masterfully baking a wide selection of breads and baked goods. Once you become familiar with bread machine settings, the possibilities for creating and experimenting are endless.

It is essential to know the features of each machine setting so that it is easier to understand which function to use.

Bread machines can be of two different types. Some brands have specific settings that cannot be changed, so it is a good idea to follow the instructions when making different types of bread to see which setting will be ideal.

Some bread machines have basic settings with times and schedules that can be changed. For example, if you notice that the bread has not risen as hoped, you can extend the rising time.

Now let us help you understand the various cycles and settings you can find on your bread machine.

BASIC CYCLE

This setting is the most commonly used function of the bread machine and allows you to create standard bread. This function generally runs for three to four hours, depending on the size of the loaf and the type of bread. You can also use this setting when making bread with whole wheat flour.

SWEET BREAD CYCLE

As the name suggests, this cycle is intended for bread with higher sugar or fat content than standard bread. This setting is also used when using ingredients such as cheese and eggs. It also allows the bread to be baked lower temperature than other functions, as the included ingredients may cause the crust to burn or darken.

NUT OR RAISIN CYCLE

Although adding ingredients such as chopped nuts and dried fruits to the pan is possible, some machines tend to chop them too finely. The nuts or raisins cycle ensures that these ingredients remain relatively finely chopped, adding texture and sweetness to the bread. This feature is ideal because it alerts you when it is time to add the nuts or fruit pieces.

WHOLE WHEAT CYCLE

Whole wheat bread needs to be kneaded and processed longer than standard loaves. That is why this cycle is perfect for bread that requires the use of this type of flour. This function allows the bread to rise enough and prevents it from becoming too dense.

FRENCH BREAD CYCLE

Most bread from Mediterranean regions, such as Italy or France, comes out much better using this function rather than the basic cycle. Many French-style loaves contain no or very little sugar.

Bread from these regions needs a longer rise time and a lower, more prolonged temperature. This allows it to create the textures and crusts we have come to love and enjoy.

DOUGH CYCLE

This cycle is perfect for making pizza dough and for making sandwiches. The machine mixes and kneads the ingredients, allowing you to remove the dough, add desired toppings or fillings, and continue baking in the traditional oven. This eliminates the need to knead on your own and reduces the need for cleanup, which is a great advantage for everyone.

RAPID BAKE CYCLE

It is dedicated to those who use quick rise yeast in their bread recipes. The rapid cycle can take anywhere from 30 minutes to two hours of the basic bread cycle, saving considerable time. Note that the rapid bake cycle varies from machine to machine.

CAKE OR QUICK CYCLE

This cycle is ideal for recipes that do not contain yeast, such as cakes. It is a primary cycle to consider when making store-bought cake and bread mixes. The bread machine does not knead the ingredients like in other cycles. It just mixes the ingredients and bakes them. This cycle and baking time may also vary from one machine to another.

JAM CYCLE

A cycle of jam on the bread machine is an absolute delight. Remember to finely chop the fruit before adding it to the bread machine for the best results. Within an hour, you can have a jar of fresh jam ready.

TIME-BAKE OR DELAYED CYCLE

This is an innovative setting that some bread machines have. It allows you to add ingredients to the bread machine and schedule the baking to start when you prefer.

CRUST FUNCTIONALITY

The crust feature of bread machines allows the user to select the crust they prefer when baking bread. Generally, there are three crust settings: soft, medium, and dark. A soft crust is always good paired with white bread varieties. On the other hand, if a crispier crust is preferred, medium and dark crusts are best. If the bread contains sweeteners, nuts, and grains, it can cause the bread to brown faster. It is therefore recommended to set a light crust.

Bread Machine Techniques

The processes in a bread machine are not very different from those used to make bread by hand. They are just less labor-intensive and less messy. The main techniques used in bread making with a bread machine are:

MIXING AND RESTING

The ingredients are mixed well and then allowed to rest before kneading.

KNEADING

This technique creates long strands of gluten. Kneading crushes, stretches, turns, and presses the dough for 20 to 30 minutes, depending on the machine and setting.

FIRST RISE

This is also called bulk fermentation. Yeast converts sugar into alcohol, which imparts flavor, and carbon dioxide, which imparts structure by swelling the gluten structure.

STIR DOWN (1 AND 2)

The paddles rotate to bring the loaf down and redistribute the dough before the second and third rising.

SECOND AND THIRD RISE

The second rising takes about 15 minutes. By the end of the third rising, the loaf will have nearly doubled in size.

BAKING

In the first 5 minutes or so of the baking process, there is a final growth of yeast in the dough and the bread becomes a finished loaf.

Main Ingredients

The ingredients needed for bread making are very simple: flour, yeast, salt, and liquid. Other ingredients add flavor, texture, and nutrition to the bread, such as sugar, fat, and eggs. Basic ingredients include:

- FLOUR. Flour is the base of the bread. The protein and gluten in flour form a network that holds the carbon dioxide and alcohol produced by yeast. Flour also provides simple sugars to feed the yeast and provides flavor, depending on the type of flour used in the recipe.

- YEAST. Yeast is a living organism that multiplies when the right amount of moisture, food, and heat is applied. As yeast multiplies rapidly, it emits carbon dioxide and ethyl alcohol. The finished bread is tastier when yeast is allowed to fulfill its life cycle completely.

- SALT. Salt strengthens gluten and slows the rising of bread by retarding the action of the yeast. Slower rising allows bread flavors to develop better and reduces the likelihood that the bread will rise too much.

- LIQUIDS. The liquid activates the yeast and dissolves the other ingredients. The most commonly used liquid is water, but ingredients such as milk can also be used. Bread made with water will have a crispier crust, but milk produces a rich, tender bread that offers more nutrition and browns more easily.

- EGGS. Eggs add protein, flavor, color, and a tender crust. Eggs contain an emulsifier, lecithin, which helps create a smooth texture, and a leavening agent, which helps the bread rise well.

- OILS AND FATS. Oils and fats add flavor, create a tender texture, and help brown the crust. Bread made with fats stays fresh longer because moisture loss in the bread is slowed. This component can also inhibit gluten formation, so the bread does not rise as much.

- SUGAR. Sugar is the food source for yeast. It also adds sweetness, tenderness, and color to the crust. Too much sugar can inhibit gluten growth or cause the dough to rise too much and collapse. Other sweeteners can replace sugar, such as honey, molasses, maple syrup, brown sugar, corn syrup, Stevia, Swerve, and erythritol.

Pro Tips

WATER TEMPERATURE

More than any other type of baking, bread making is a science, and every detail matters. The ingredient that determines the leavening of bread and, thus, its success is yeast. Since yeast is a living organism, it does its job correctly only under certain specific conditions. This is why the temperature of the water is so important. If the water is too cold, the yeast will be slow and will not produce enough carbon dioxide. This will lead to loaves of bread that do not rise enough and have a thick, doughy texture. If the water is too warm, the yeast will be killed. For best results, you should use a kitchen thermometer and make sure the water is between 115°F and 125°F. Water heated in this range provides the perfect environment for the yeast to activate and work. Also, be sure to keep track of the age of your yeast. Since it is a living organism, it will eventually die and no longer be able to produce carbon dioxide. All yeast packages have an expiration date. If your yeast has passed or is near that date, throw it away and buy fresh yeast.

MOISTURE OF THE DOUGH

In order to get the best results in bread making, it is important to ensure that the dough has the correct moisture content. This affects the leavening and even baking of the bread. While kneading, check the dough. If it is mushy and not holding together, add some flour until the consistency becomes firmer. Also, add some flour if the dough feels sticky to the touch or if the dough pulls away from your fingers when you touch it. Conversely, if the dough feels flaky or floury to the touch, add a little water until it becomes smooth and elastic.

How to tell if the dough is perfect: Prick it with your finger. Ideally, the dough should bounce quickly when you poke it.

EXPERIMENT WITH FLOURS

In addition to all-purpose flour, you can also experiment with whole-wheat flour, which will give a dense, nutty flavor and an excellent source of nutrition. By experimenting with different ratios of whole wheat flour to all-purpose flour, you can customize the perfect level of whole wheat flour, from a light hint to a very dense and nutritious loaf. You can also purchase rye flour to mix with all-purpose flour to make a hearty and flavorful rye bread. Adding a tablespoon of caraway seeds makes a genuinely authentic rye bread. Since there is a wide variety of different flours on the market today, you can experiment with adding many different types of flour. We recommend adding small amounts of nut flour, such as almond or coconut flour, for an extra flavor.

CHOOSING THE RIGHT TYPE OF YEAST

There are many types of yeast, and choosing the right one can be a challenge. Yeast is a natural organism, and the main ingredient bakers use to produce leavened bread.

The best type of yeast to use for most bread machine applications is quick rising yeast. It differs from traditional active dry yeast because it activates even faster and produces carbon dioxide at a faster rate.

BREAD FLOUR Vs. ALL PURPOSE FLOUR

Just as there are different types of yeast, there are different types of flour that produce different types of bread. In general, bread flour is recommended when baking in the bread machine, but depending on the kind of loaf you want to make, this is not always the case.

Bread flour is higher in protein than all-purpose flour, and as a result, bread made with bread flour has a higher gluten content. The result is that the loaves are more chewy and dense than those prepared with all-purpose flour. Therefore, if you want to make a chewy French loaf, bread flour is definitely the right choice. However, classic white bread or brioche can be lighter and fluffier with all-purpose flour.

MAKE PASTA WITH YOUR BREAD MACHINE

While you won't be baking the pasta in the bread maker, you can take advantage of its powerful motor to take a lot of the effort out of making fresh pasta. Because pasta dough needs extensive kneading to come out smooth and even, you can place all of your pasta dough ingredients (flour, eggs, salt, and a bit of olive oil) into the baking pan and use the dough/pasta function for kneading your dough to perfection effortlessly. When it is finished kneading, remove the dough from the machine and wrap in plastic wrap. Place the dough on a countertop and allow to rest for about half an hour. This will give the ingredients time to fully incorporate before you roll it and cut it.

ADDING INGREDIENTS TO THE BREAD

Once the bread machine has combined the bread ingredients, you will have the opportunity to add different ingredients to the dough. Chopped nuts and dried fruit are great additions and give the bread an interesting flavor and texture. You can also try adding chopped olives and fresh herbs to make delicious loaves that work wonderfully as a sandwich base or healthy snack. Another fun way to add ingredients to bread is to make sweet breads such as cinnamon and raisin or cranberry. Just sprinkle a little cinnamon mixed with sugar and a handful of raisins, or add dried cranberries with a teaspoon of fresh orange zest.

Once you start using your bread machine, you will find that the possibilities for making fantastic, healthy, and creative breads are almost limitless.

Savory Bread

Cheesy Bread

Preparation Time: 10 minutes
Cooking Time: 4 hours
Servings: 12 slices

Ingredients:

- *1/4 cup butter, unsalted*
- *1 cup+3 tbsp. cream cheese, softened*
- *4 egg yolks*
- *1 tsp. vanilla extract*
- *1 tsp. baking powder*
- *1/4 tsp. sea salt*
- *2 tbsp. monk fruit powder*
- *1/2 cup peanut flour*

Directions: Add butter and cream cheese until combined. Then mix well in egg yolks, vanilla, baking powder, salt, and monk fruit powder. Add the egg mixture to the bread bucket. Top with flour and shut the lid. Select the BASIC/WHITE cycle and press START.
Remove the bread when done. Cool, slice, and serve.

Nutrition: Calories: 95.8; Fat: 7.4 g; Carbs: 2.1 g; Protein: 5.5 g

Almond Meal Bread

Preparation Time: 10 minutes
Cooking Time: 4 hours
Servings: 10 slices

Ingredients:

- *4 eggs*
- *1/4 cup coconut oil, melted*
- *1 tbsp. apple cider vinegar*
- *2 1/4 cups almond meal*
- *1 tsp. baking soda*
- *1/4 cup flaxseed meal, ground*
- *1 tsp. onion powder*
- *1 tbsp. garlic, minced*
- *1 tsp. sea salt*
- *1 tsp. sage leaves, chopped*
- *1 tsp. fresh thyme*
- *1 tsp. rosemary leaves, chopped*

Directions: In a bowl, beat eggs, coconut oil, and vinegar until mixed.
In another bowl, place an almond meal and add the remaining ingredients. Mix well.
Add the egg mixture into the bread bucket, and top with flour mixture. Cover the lid.
Select the BASIC/WHITE cycle. Press START. Remove the bread when done.
Cool, slice, and serve.

Nutrition: Calories: 102.5; Fat: 8.5 g; Carbs: 1.5 g; Protein: 5.4 g

Macadamia Butter Bread

Preparation Time: 10 minutes
Cooking Time: 4 hours
Servings: 8 slices

Ingredients:

- *1 cup natural macadamia nut butter*
- *5 eggs*
- *1/2 tsp. apple cider vinegar*
- *1/4 cup coconut flour*
- *1/2 tsp. baking soda*

Directions: Mix macadamia nut butter, eggs, and vanilla and mix until smooth.
Stir in flour and baking soda and mix well. Add the batter into the bread bucket and cover.
Select BASIC/WHITE cycle. Press START. Remove the bread when done.
Cool, slice, and serve.

Nutrition: Calories: 152.3; Fat: 11.2 g; Carbs: 3.2 g; Protein: 7.8 g

3-Seed Bread

Preparation Time: 10 minutes
Cooking Time: 4 hours
Servings: 18 slices

Ingredients:

- *2 eggs*
- *1/4 cup butter, melted*
- *1 cup warm water (100°F)*
- *1/4 cup chia seeds*
- *1/2 cup pumpkin seeds*
- *1/2 cup sunflower seeds*
- *1/2 cup psyllium husks*
- *1/4 cup coconut flour*
- *1/4 tsp. salt*
- *1 tsp. baking powder*

Directions: Beat eggs and butter in a bowl until well blended.
Add flour to another bowl. Then mix the remaining ingredients except for water until mixed.
Pour water into the bread bucket, add the egg mixture, and top with the flour mixture. Cover.
Select the BASIC/WHITE cycle. Press START.
Remove the bread when done. Cool, slice, and serve.

Nutrition: Calories: 137.5; Fat: 8.4 g; Carbs: 5.1 g; Protein: 6.5 g

Cheesy Garlic Bread

Preparation Time: 10 minutes
Cooking Time: 4 hours
Servings: 16 slices

Ingredients:

- *5 eggs*
- *2 cups almond flour*
- *1/2 tsp. xanthan gum*
- *1 tsp. garlic powder*
- *1 tsp. salt*
- *1 tsp. parsley*
- *1 tsp. Italian seasoning*
- *1 tsp. oregano, dried*
- *1 stick unsalted butter, melted*
- *1 cup mozzarella cheese, grated*
- *2 tbsp. ricotta cheese*
- *1 cup cheddar cheese, grated*
- *1/3 cup parmesan cheese, grated*

For the topping:

- *1/2 stick unsalted butter, melted*
- *1 tsp. garlic powder*

Directions: Whisk the eggs in a bowl. Place flour in another bowl. Stir in xanthan gum and all the cheeses until well combined. Place butter in a bowl and add all the seasonings to it. Mix well.
Add the egg mixture into the bread bucket. Then add the seasoning mixture and flour mixture. Cover.
Select the BASIC/WHITE cycle. Press START.
Remove the bread when done. Cool, slice, and serve.

Nutrition: Calories: 247.8; Fat: 12.5 g; Carbs: 1.1 g; Protein: 9.2 g

Cumin Bread

Preparation Time: 10 minutes
Cooking Time: 4 hours
Servings: 12 slices

Ingredients:

- *2 eggs*
- *1 1/2 tbsp. olive oil*
- *2/3 cup milk*
- *2 tbsp. Picante sauce*
- *2 1/2 cusp flour*
- *1/4 tsp. salt*
- *2 tsp. active dry yeast*
- *1/4 tsp. mustard powder*
- *2 tsp. cumin, ground*

Directions: Beat eggs until frothy, then beat in oil, milk, and sauce until combined.
Place flour in another bowl, stir in the remaining ingredients, and mix.
Add egg mixture into the bread bucket, top with flour, and then cover.
Select the BASIC/WHITE cycle. PRESS START.
Remove the bread when done. Cool, slice, and serve.

Nutrition: Calories: 105.4; Fat: 6.3 g; Carbs: 3.4 g ; Protein: 4.5 g

Rosemary Bread

Preparation Time: 10 minutes
Cooking Time: 4 hours
Servings: 10 slices

Ingredients:

- *6 eggs*
- *8 tbsp. unsalted butter, melted*
- *1/2 cup flour*
- *1 tsp. baking powder*
- *1/4 tsp. salt*
- *1/2 tsp. onion powder*
- *1 tsp. garlic powder*
- *2 tsp. rosemary, dried*

Directions: Gently mix eggs and butter until well combined.

Place flour in another bowl. Stir in the remaining ingredients until mixed.
Add egg mixture into the bread bucket and top with flour mixture. Cover.
Select the BASIC/WHITE cycle. Press START.
Remove the bread when done. Cool, slice, and serve.

Nutrition: Calories: 144.4 Fat: 11.5 g; Carbs: 2.5 g ; Protein: 5.6 g

Sesame and Flaxseed Bread

Preparation Time: 10 minutes
Cooking Time: 4 minutes
Servings: 10 slices

Ingredients:

- *3 eggs*
- *1/2 cup cream cheese, softened*
- *6 1/2 tbsp. heavy whipping cream*
- *1/4 cup coconut oil, melted*
- *1/2 cup almond flour*
- *1/4 cup flaxseed*
- *6 1/2 tbsp. coconut flour*
- *2 2/3 tbsp. sesame seeds*
- *1/2 tsp. salt*
- *1 1/2 tsp. baking powder*
- *2 tbsp. psyllium husk powder, ground*
- *1/2 tsp. Caraway seeds, ground*

Directions: Beat the eggs, cream cheese, whipping cream, and coconut oil until mixed.
Add flours to another bowl. Then mix the remaining ingredients and mix.
Add egg mixture into the bread bucket, then top with flour mixture. Cover.
Select the BASIC/WHITE cycle. Press START.
Remove the bread when done. Cool, slice, and serve.

Nutrition: Calories: 257.5; Fat: 20.1 g; Carbs: 5.2 g ; Protein: 8.3 g

Bacon and Cheddar Bread

Preparation Time: 10 minutes
Cooking Time: 4 hours
Servings: 9 slices

Ingredients:

- *2 eggs*
- *1/4 cup beer*
- *2 tbsp. unsalted butter, melted*
- *1/4 cup bacon, cooked and crumbled*
- *1/2 cup cheddar cheese, shredded*
- *1 cup and 1/2 tbsp. flour*
- *1/4 tsp. salt*
- *1/2 tbsp. baking powder*

Directions: Blend eggs, beer, and butter in a bowl. Fold in the bacon and cheese until just mixed.
Add egg mixture into the bread bucket. Top with flour mixture (flour mixed with dry ingredients) and cover.

Select the BASIC/WHITE cycle and press START.
Remove the bread when done. Cool, slice, and serve.

Nutrition: Calories: 138.4; Fat: 10.2 g; Carbs: 2.2 g; Protein: 6.7 g

Olive Bread

Preparation Time: 10 minutes
Cooking Time: 4 hours
Servings: 10 slices

Ingredients:

- *4 eggs*
- *4 tbsp. avocado oil*
- *1 tbsp. apple cider vinegar*
- *1/2 cup flour*
- *2 1/2 tsp. active dry yeast*
- *1 1/2 tbsp. rosemary, dried*
- *1/2 tsp. salt*
- *1/3 cup black olives, chopped*
- *1/2 cup boiling water*

Directions: Stir oil in vinegar and fold in the olives.
Place the flour in another bowl, and stir in yeast, salt, and rosemary until mixed. Add the warm water and gently mix.
Add olives into the bread bucket, top with flour mixture, and cover.
Select the BASIC/WHITE cycle. Then press START.
Remove the bread when done. Cool, slice, and serve.

Nutrition: Calories: 80.5; Fat: 4.5 g; Carbs: 2.2 g; Protein: 4.2 g

Jalapeño Cheese Bread

Preparation Time: 10 minutes
Cooking Time: 4 hours
Servings: 8 slices

Ingredients:

- *2 tbsp. Greek yogurt, full-fat*
- *4 eggs*
- *1/3 cup flour*
- *1/2 tsp. sea salt*
- *2 tbsp. whole psyllium husks*
- *1 tsp. active dry yeast*
- *1/4 cup jalapeños, diced and pickled*
- *1/4 cup cheddar cheese, shredded and divided*

Directions: Beat yogurt and egg in a bowl.
Place the flour in another bowl. Add the remaining ingredients and mix well.
Add egg mixture into the bread bucket, top with flour mixture, and cover.

Select the BASIC/WHITE cycle and press START.
Remove the bread when done. Cool, slice, and serve.

Nutrition: Calories: 103.1; Fat: 6.1 g; Carbs: 2.4 g; Protein: 6.8 g

Dill and Cheddar Bread

Preparation Time: 10 minutes
Cooking Time: 4 hours
Servings: 10 slices

Ingredients:

- *4 eggs*
- *1/4 tsp. sour cream*
- *5 tbsp. unsalted butter*
- *2 cups cheddar cheese, grated*
- *1 1/2 cups flour*
- *1 scoop egg white*
- *1/4 tsp. salt*
- *1 tsp. garlic powder*
- *4 tsp. baking powder*
- *1/4 tbsp. dill, dried, and weed*

Directions: Beat eggs, sour cream, butter, and cheese until just mixed.
Place flour in another bowl. Then stir in egg white protein, salt, garlic powder, baking powder, and dill and mix.
Add the egg mixture into the bread bucket, and top with the flour mixture. Cover.
Select the BASIC/WHITE cycle and press START.
Remove the bread when done. Cool, slice, and serve.

Nutrition: Calories: 290.2; Fat: 21.2 g; Carbs: 5.1 g; Protein: 15.3 g

Mozzarella and Cream Cheese Bread

Preparation Time: 10 minutes
Cooking Time: 4 hours
Servings: 8 slices

Ingredients:

- *3/4 cup mozzarella cheese, shredded*
- *1/4 cup cream cheese, softened*
- *1 egg*
- *1/3 cup almond flour*
- *1/4 tsp. garlic powder*
- *2 tsp. baking powder*
- *1/2 tsp. Italian seasoning*
- *1/2 cup cheddar cheese, shredded*

Directions: Melt the mozzarella cheese and cream cheese in the microwave.
Beat the egg in another bowl. Place flour in another bowl, add the remaining ingredients and mix.

Add blended egg into the bread bucket, top with melted cheese mixture, and then with flour mixture. Cover.
Select the BASIC/WHITE cycle. Press START.
Remove the bread when done. Cool, slice, and serve.

Nutrition: Calories: 168.5; Fat: 12.5 g; Carbs: 1.4 g ; Protein: 4.3 g

Sourdough Dough

Preparation Time: 10 minutes
Cooking Time: 4 hours
Servings: 15

Ingredients:

- *2 eggs*
- *6 egg whites*
- *3/4 cup milk*
- *1/4 cup apple cider vinegar*
- *1/2 cup of warm water (100°F)*
- *2 cups flour*
- *1/2 cup flaxseed, ground*
- *1 tsp. salt*
- *1 tsp. baking soda*
- *1/3 cup psyllium powder*

Directions: In a bowl, add eggs, egg white, milk, vinegar, and water and whisk until combined.
In another bowl, place flour and stir in the remaining ingredients until mixed.
Add the egg mixture into the bread bucket, top with the flour mixture, and cover.
Select the BASIC/WHITE cycle. Press START.
Remove the bread when done. Cool, slice, and serve.

Nutrition: Calories: 113.5; Fat: 7.8 g; Carbs: 4.5 g; Protein: 6.5 g

Cheddar and Herb Bread

Preparation Time: 10 minutes
Cooking Time: 4 hours
Servings: 16 slices

Ingredients:

- *6 eggs*
- *1/2 cup unsalted butter, softened*
- *2 cups flour*
- *1 tsp. baking powder*
- *2 tbsp. garlic powder*
- *1/2 tsp. salt*
- *1 tbsp. parsley, dried*
- *1/2 tbsp. oregano, dried*
- *1 1/2 cups cheddar cheese, shredded*

Directions: Beat eggs until frothy and then beat in the butter until combined.
Place flour in another bowl. Stir in remaining ingredients until mixed.
Add egg mixture into the bread bucket, top with flour mixture, and cover.
Select the BASIC/WHITE cycle and press START.
Remove the bread when done. Cool, slice, and serve.

Nutrition: Calories: 205.2; Fat: 15.5 g; Carbs: 4.5 g ; Protein: 8.2 g

Basil Parmesan Slices

Preparation Time: 10 minutes
Cooking Time: 3 hours and 25 minutes
Servings: 16 slices

Ingredients:

- *1 cup water*
- *1/2 cup parmesan cheese, grated*
- *3 tbsp. granulated sugar*
- *1 tbsp. basil, dried*
- *1 1/2 tbsp. olive oil*
- *1 tsp. salt*
- *3 cups flour*
- *2 tsp. active dry yeast*

Directions: Place everything in the bread machine according to the bread machine's recommendation. Select BASIC and press START. Remove the bread when done. Cool, slice, and serve.

Nutrition: Calories: 95.2; Fat: 6.8 g; Carbs: 6.7 g; Protein: 8.6 g

Creamy Rolls

Preparation Time: 20 minutes
Cooking Time: 30 minutes
Servings: 6

Ingredients:

- *3 eggs*
- *1/8 tsp. sour cream*
- *3 oz. cream cheese*
- *1/8 tsp. salt*

Directions: Preheat the oven to 300°F. Separate the egg yolks and the egg whites.
Whip the egg whites with the sour cream and form soft peaks.
Mix the egg yolks, cream cheese, and salt in another bowl.
Fold the egg whites into the egg yolk mixture.
Pour the batter into a greased pan and bake in the preheated oven for 30 minutes.
Cool for 5 minutes and serve.

Nutrition: Calories: 108.9; Fat: 8.4 g; Carbs: 0.7 g; Protein: 7.2 g

Ricotta Chive Bread

Preparation Time: 5 minutes
Cooking Time: 3 hours
Servings: 1 loaf

Ingredients:

- *1 cup lukewarm water*

- *1/3 cup whole or part-skim ricotta cheese*
- *1 1/2 tsp. salt*
- *1 tbsp. granulated sugar*
- *3 cups bread flour*
- *1/2 cup chives, chopped*
- *2 1/2 tsp. instant yeast*

Directions: Add ingredients to the bread machine pan except for dried fruit. Choose a basic bread setting and light/medium crust.

Nutrition: Calories 90.2; Carbs 15.7 g; Protein 4.3 g

Bread with Walnuts and Garlic

Preparation Time: 4 hours
Servings: 10

Ingredients:

- *3 cups flour*
- *2 tsp. dry yeast*
- *1 cup walnuts*
- *10 garlic cloves, chopped*
- *10 tbsp. olive oil*
- *1 cup garlic butter, melted*
- *2 cups water*
- *2 tsp. sugar*
- *2 egg yolks*
- *Sea salt to taste*

Directions: Preheat the oven to 290°F–320°F and roast the walnuts for 10–15 minutes until lightly browned and crispy. Set aside to cool completely. Grind the walnuts using a food processor.
Melt the unsalted butter softer, take it out of the fridge and leave it for around 30 minutes, or melt the butter using a frying pan. Meanwhile, chop the garlic cloves.
Put the flour into the bowl and add yeast, sugar, garlic, egg yolks, olive oil, and sea salt. Mix until there are a smooth consistency and homogenous mass. Add in the walnuts.
Spoon the mixture into the bread machine, add in the water and melted softened garlic butter, and mix well.
Lubricate the surface of the dough with water or the egg yolk.
Now close the lid and turn the bread machine on the basic/white bread program.
After the bread is ready, take it out and leave for 1 hour covered with the towel, then slice and serve.

Nutrition: Calories 98.7; Fat 3.4 g; Carbs 4.4 g; Protein 2.2 g

Almond Bread with Hazelnuts and Garlic

Preparation time: 25 minutes
Cooking time: 0
Servings: 8

Ingredients:

- *10 garlic cloves, chopped*
- *1 cup hazelnuts*
- *3 cups almond flour*
- *2 tsp. dry yeast*
- *1 cup garlic butter, melted*
- *2 tsp. sugar*
- *10 tbsp. olive oil*
- *2 cups water*
- *2 egg yolks*
- *Sea salt, to taste*

Directions: Preheat the oven to 300°F–320°F and roast the hazelnuts for 10–15 minutes until lightly browned and crispy. Keep aside to cool wholly. Blend the hazelnuts using a food processor.
Melt the butter using a frying pan. Chop the garlic cloves.
Put the almond flour into the bowl and then add in the yeast, sugar, garlic, egg yolks, olive oil, and sea salt and mix until there is a smooth consistency. Add in the hazelnuts.
Spoon the mixture into the bread machine, add in the water and melted softened garlic butter, and mix well.
Lubricate the surface of the dough with water or the egg yolk.
Now close the lid and turn the bread machine on the basic/white bread program.
Allow to cool or place in refrigerator and then enjoy it.

Nutrition: Calories 112.3; Fat 1.2 g; Carbs 3.7 g; Protein 6.5 g

Herb Blend Bread

Preparation Time: 40 minutes
Cooking Time: 40 minutes
Servings: 16

Ingredients:

- *1 1/2 cup almond flour*
- *1 cup parmesan cheese*
- *3/4 tsp. baking powder*
- *3 eggs*
- *3 tbsp. oil*
- *1/2 tbsp. rosemary*
- *1/2 tsp. thyme, ground*
- *1/2 tsp. sage, ground*
- *1/2 tsp. oregano*
- *1/2 tsp. garlic powder*
- *1/2 tsp. onion powder*
- *1/4 tsp. salt*

Directions: Light beat eggs and oil together before adding to the bread machine pan.
Add all the remaining ingredients to the bread machine pan.
Set the bread machine to the gluten-free setting. When it is done, remove the pan from the bread machine.
Let cool slightly before transferring to a cooling rack.

Nutrition: Calories 168.7; Carbs 5.6 g; Fat 14.5 g; Protein 11.9 g

Herbed Garlic Bread

Preparation Time: 10 minutes
Cooking Time: 45 minutes
Servings: 10

Ingredients:

- *1/2 cup flour*
- *8 tbsp. melted butter cooled*
- *1 tsp. baking powder*
- *6 large eggs*
- *1 tsp. garlic powder*
- *1 tsp. rosemary, dried*
- *1/4 tsp. salt*
- *1/2 tsp. onion powder*

Directions: Prepare bread machine loaf pan, greasing it with cooking spray.
In a bowl, add flour, baking powder, onion, garlic, rosemary, and salt into a bowl. Combine and mix well.
Into another bowl, add eggs, and beat until bubbly on top.
Add melted butter into the bowl with the eggs and beat until mixed.
Following the instructions in the machine's manual, mix the dry ingredients with the wet ingredients and pour into the bread machine loaf pan, taking care to follow how to mix in the baking powder.
Add the bread pan to the machine, and select the basic bread setting - together with the bread size and crust type if available - then press start once you have closed the lid of the machine.
When the bread is ready, remove the bread pan from the machine using oven mitts.
Let it cool before slicing.

Nutrition: Calories 145.7; Fat 10.5 g; Carbs 2.5 g; Protein 6.6 g

Beet Bread

Preparation Time: 35 minutes
Cooking Time: 35 minutes
Servings: 6

Ingredients:

- *1 cup warm water*
- *3 1/2 cups flour*
- *1 1/2 cups beet puree*
- *2 tbsp. olive oil*
- *A pinch of salt*
- *1 tsp. stevia*
- *1 tsp. baking powder*
- *1 tsp. baking soda*

Directions: Add all ingredients gradually in the bread machine's pan, following the manufacturer's instructions for mixing dry and wet ingredients. Set the bread machine to the basic setting.
When done, remove the bread machine pan from the bread machine.
Let cool slightly before transferring to a cooling rack. Cool the bread down, slice, and serve.

Nutrition: Calories 198.8; Fat 6.8 g; Carbs 4.5 g; Protein 8.6 g

Hot Red Pepper Bread

Preparation Time: 15 minutes
Cooking Time: 1 hour
Servings: 12

Ingredients:

- *2 cups hot red peppers, roasted, dried, and crushed*
- *2 tsp. active dry yeast*
- *1 tsp. pepper powder*
- *2 eggs*
- *2 tsp. warm water*
- *1/2 cup milk*
- *1/2 tsp. salt*
- *1 1/2 tsp. baking powder*
- *3 cups flour*
- *2 tsp. unsalted butter, melted*

Directions: Get a mixing container and combine the flour, dried and crushed roasted hot red peppers, salt, and baking powder.
Get another mixing container and combine the eggs, milk, warm water, and melted unsalted butter.
As per the instructions in the machine manual, pour the ingredients in the bread pan, following the instructions on how to mix the yeast.
Place the bread pan into the machine, and select the sweet bread setting, together with the bread size and crust type, if available, then press start once you have closed the lid of the machine.
When the bread is ready, extract it, and place it on a metallic mesh surface to cool completely before cutting.

Nutrition: Calories 105.7; Fat 5.1 g; Carbs 7.2g; Protein 12.6

Herbed Keto Bread

Preparation Time: 5 minutes
Cooking Time: 40 minutes
Servings: 8

Ingredients:

- *3 cups coconut flour*
- *1 tsp. baking powder*
- *1 tsp. baking soda*
- *2 tsp. stevia*
- *1 1/2 cups warm water*
- *1/2 tsp. basil, dried*
- *1 tsp. oregano, dried*
- *1/2 tsp. thyme, dried*
- *1/2 tsp. marjoram, dried*
- *2 tbsp. olive oil*

Directions: In a bowl, mix the flour with baking powder, baking soda, stevia, basil, oregano, thyme, and marjoram, and stir.
Put the rest of the ingredients, stir well, and transfer the dough to the bread machine loaf pan pre-greased with cooking spray. However, look at the manufacturer's instructions for mixing dry and wet ingredients.
Put the bread pan into the machine, and select the basic bread setting - together with the bread size if available - then press start once you have closed the lid of the machine.
When the bread is ready, remove the bread pan from the machine using oven mitts.
Cool the bread down before serving.

Nutrition: Calories 189.4; Fat 5.7 g; Carbs 4.5 g; Protein 7.6 g

Pizza Crusts

Preparation Time: 10 minutes
Cooking Time: 5-10 minutes
Servings: 2 slices

Ingredients:

For the dough:

- *5 whole eggs and 3 egg whites*
- *1/2 tsp. baking powder*
- *1/4 cup flour, sifted with more for dusting*
- *Salt, pepper, Italian spices*

For the sauce:

- *2 garlic cloves, minced*
- *1/2 cup organic tomato sauce*
- *1 tsp. basil, dried*
- *1/4 tsp. pink sea salt*

Directions: Preheat oven to 350°F.
Add all dough ingredients to the bread machine pan following the order in the bread machine's manual instructions.
Put the bread pan in the machine, and select the dough cycle setting, or specific pizza program, if available. Then press start once you have closed the lid of the machine.
Remove the dough from the bread machine when the cycle is complete.
Lightly grease a small pan and place over medium-low heat. Pour some of the batters evenly once the pan is hot.
Cover and let cook in the oven for about 3–5 minutes or until bubbles form on top. Flip the other side and cook for 2 minutes. Transfer to a platter and repeat this for the remaining batter.
Once the crusts are cool, use a fork to poke holes on the crusts roughly. This will help them cook evenly. Lightly dust with coconut flour and set aside.
For the sauce, whisk all the ingredients together, then let stand for 30 minutes to allow thickening.
Spread the pizza bases with the sauce and top with your favorite topping. Bake for about 3–5 minutes or until done.

Nutrition: Calories: 123.5; Fat: 0.5 g; Carbs: 4.6 g; Fiber: 2.3 g; Protein: 9.8 g

Keto Pizza Crust

Preparation Time: 10 minutes
Cooking Time: 7-10 minutes
Servings: 2 slices

Ingredients:

- *100 g. almond flour, blanched*
- *3 tbsp. coconut flour*
- *2 tapioca flour*
- *2 tsp. baking powder*
- *1/4 tsp. pink sea salt*
- *2 tsp. apple cider vinegar*
- *1/4 cup water*
- *1 egg*

Directions: Put all ingredients into the bread machine pan fruit following the order in the bread machine's manual instructions. Put the bread pan into the machine, and select the dough cycle setting, or specific pizza program, if available. Then press start once you have closed the lid of the machine. Remove the dough from the bread machine when the cycle is complete. Preheat the oven to 350°F and line a baking tray with parchment paper. Flatten the dough, spread it on the prepared tray, and bake for 7 minutes on each side. Top with your favorite topping and return to the oven for about 3–5 more minutes.

Nutrition: Calories: 115.8; Fat: 7.9 g; Carbs: 4.6 g; Protein: 6.5 g

Keto Breadsticks

Preparation Time: 6 minutes
Cooking Time: 30 minutes
Servings: 15 slices

Ingredients:

- *2 cups (8 oz.) mozzarella cheese*
- *3/4 cup (3 oz.) cheddar cheese*
- *3/4 cup almond flour*
- *1 tbsp. psyllium husk powder*
- *3 tbsp. (1.5 oz.) cream cheese*
- *1 large egg*
- *1 tsp. baking powder*

Directions: Preheat stove to 400°F.
Combine egg, cream cheese, and cheddar until somewhat joined. In another bowl, consolidate all the dry fixings following the order in the bread machine's manual instructions.
Measure out the mozzarella cheese and microwave in 20-second interims until sizzling.
Add the egg, cream cheddar, and dry fixings into the mozzarella cheese and combine.
Pour mixture into the bread machine loaf pan.
Put the bread pan into the machine, and select the breadstick setting. If not available, use cookies or pasta dough program. Then press start once you have closed the lid of the machine.
Remove the dough from the machine when the cycle is complete.
Divide the dough into 15 equal pieces and roll them with the hands forming breadsticks.
At that point, season the mixture with the flavorings you like.
Place the breadsticks on the baking sheet and brush with the egg yolks.
Bake 13–15 minutes on top rack until fresh. Serve while warm.

Nutrition: Calories: 58.7; Carbs: 3.4 g; Fiber: 2.5 g; Fat: 4.6 g; Protein: 5.4 g

Cheesy Breadsticks

Preparation Time: 10 minutes
Cooking Time: 15 minutes
Servings: 8

Ingredients:

For the breadsticks:

- *1/2 cup parmesan cheese, shredded*
- *1 cups mozzarella cheese, shredded*
- *1/2 tsp. garlic powder*
- *1 tsp. Italian seasoning*
- *1/4 tsp. baking powder*
- *1/2 tsp. salt*

- *4 eggs*
- *1 oz. cream cheese, softened*
- *1/3 cup flour*
- *4 1/2 tbsp. butter, melted and cooled*

For the top:

- *12 tsp. Italian spices*
- *1/4 cup parmesan cheese, shredded*
- *2 cups mozzarella cheese, shredded*

Directions: Preheat the oven to 400°F. Prepare a 7x11 baking pan by greasing it with cooking spray. Combine the cream cheese, salt, eggs, and melted butter, then mix.
Add the spices, baking powder, and flour to the butter mixture and stir until combined, then stir in the parmesan and mozzarella. Pour mixture into the bread machine loaf pan.
Put the bread pan into the machine, and select the breadstick setting. If not available use cookies or pasta dough program. Then press start once you have closed the lid of the machine.
Remove the dough from the machine when the cycle is complete.
Transfer the batter to a casserole dish, then top with the additional Italian spices, parmesan cheese, and mozzarella.
Bake until the breadsticks are done for 15 minutes. Halfway through baking, use a pizza cutter to create individual breadsticks.
Transfer the pan to the top rack of the oven and broil until the cheese is bubbly and brown for around 1–2 minutes.

Nutrition: Calories: 297.9; Carbs: 2.4 g; Fat: 21.3 g; Protein: 18.7 g

Low Carbs Yeast Bread

Preparation Time: 10 minutes
Cooking Time: 4 hours
Servings: 16 slices

Ingredients:

- *1 tsp. salt*
- *4 tbsp. oat flour*
- *1 package dry yeast rapid rise/highly active*
- *1 1/2 tsp. baking powder*
- *1/2 tsp. sugar*
- *1 1/8 cups warm water*
- *1/4 cup coarse unprocessed wheat bran*
- *3 tbsp. olive oil*
- *1/4 cup flax meal*
- *1 cup vital wheat gluten flour*
- *3/4 cup soy flour*

Directions: Add water, sugar, and yeast to the bread machine and let rest there for 10 minutes.
Add the remaining ingredients and select bread mode on the machine.
When the cooking time is over, remove the bread from the machine and let it rest for about 10 minutes.

Nutrition: Calories 97.9; Fat 4.5 g; Carbs 5.7 g; Protein 11.9 g

Seeded Bread

Preparation Time: 10 minutes
Cooking Time: 40 minutes
Servings: 16 slices

Ingredients:

- *2 tbsp. chia seeds*
- *1/4 tsp. salt*
- *7 large eggs*
- *1/2 tsp. xanthan gum*
- *2 cups flour*
- *1 tsp. baking powder*
- *1/2 cup unsalted butter*
- *3 tbsp. sesame seeds*
- *2 tbsp. olive oil*

Directions: Put the ingredients into the bread machine.
Close the lid and choose bread mode. Once done, take out from the machine and cut into at least 16 slices.
This seeded bread can be kept in the fridge for up to 4–5 days.

Nutrition: Calories 100.2; Fat 15.6 g; Carbs 3.4 g; Protein 7.6 g

Nut and Seed Bread

Preparation Time: 35 minutes
Cooking Time: 45 minutes
Servings: 16 slices

Ingredients:

- *1 cup pumpkin seeds*
- *1 tsp. salt*
- *1/2 cup flour*
- *4 eggs, whisked*
- *1/2 cup whole almonds*
- *1 tbsp. lemon juice*
- *1 cup raw pecans*
- *1/4 cup olive oil*
- *1/2 cup hazelnuts*
- *1/4 cup poppy seeds*
- *1/2 cup flax meal*
- *1 cup sunflower seeds*
- *1/2 cup chia seeds*

Directions: Put all the ingredients into the bread machine.
Close the lid and choose bread mode. Once done, take out from the machine and cut into at least 16 slices.

Nutrition: Calories 315.6; Fat 25.8 g; Carbs 10.1 g; Protein 13.1 g

Almond Bread Loaf

Preparation Time: 10 minutes
Cooking Time: 3 hours and 22 minutes
Servings: 15

Ingredients:

- *2 1/2 cups almond flour*
- *1/3 cup coconut flour*
- *1/2 tsp. xanthan gum*
- *1 1/2 tsp. baking powder*
- *1/4 tsp. salt*
- *Sesame seeds*
- *1/4 cup butter, melted and cooled*
- *5 eggs*
- *2/3 cup almond milk*
- *1/4 tsp. tartar cream*

Directions: Put all the ingredients into the bread machine.
Close the lid and choose bread mode. Once done, cut out from the machine into at least 16 slices.

Nutrition: Calories 214.5; Fat 8.1 g; Carbs 3.5 g; Protein 27.2 g

Collagen Bread

Preparation Time: 10 minutes
Cooking Time: 3 hours and 22 minutes
Servings: 12

Ingredients:

- *6 tbsp. almond flour*
- *1/2 cup collagen protein, unflavored*
- *1 tsp. baking powder*
- *1 tsp. xanthan gum*
- *A pinch of pink salt*
- *5 eggs, separated*
- *1 tbsp. coconut oil, unflavored and liquid*

Directions: Put all the ingredients into the bread machine.
Close the lid and choose bread mode. Once done, cut out from the machine into at least 16 slices.

Nutrition: Calories 75.7; Fat 4.5 g; Carbs 0.7 g; Protein 8.7 g

Macadamia Bread

Preparation Time: 10 minutes
Cooking Time: 60minutes
Servings: 8

Ingredients:

- *1/4 cup flour*
- *1 cup macadamia nuts*
- *2 tbsp. flax meal*
- *1 tsp. baking powder*
- *2 scoops of whey protein powder*
- *4 eggs*
- *2 egg whites*
- *1 tbsp. lemon juice*
- *1/4 cup butter, melted*

Directions: Put all the ingredients into the bread machine. Close the lid and choose express bake mode. Once done, cut out from the machine into at least 16 slices.

Nutrition: Calories 255.7; Fat 20.4 g; Carbs 4.1 g; Protein 12.5 g

Almond Bacon Bread

Preparation Time: 10 minutes
Cooking Time: 3 hours and 18 minutes
Servings: 10

Ingredients:

- *1 1/2 cups almond flour*
- *1 tbsp. baking powder*
- *7 oz. bacon, diced*
- *2 eggs*
- *1 1/2 cups cheddar cheese, shredded*
- *4 tbsp. butter, melted*
- *1/3 cup sour cream*

Directions: Put all ingredients into the bread machine. Close the lid and choose the sweet bread mode. When cooking is over, remove the bread from the machine and let it rest for about 10 minutes.

Nutrition: Calories 305.7; Fat 24.6 g; Carbs 2.3 g; Protein 15.4 g

Bread with Beef and Peanuts

Preparation Time: 3 hours
Cooking Time: 20 minutes
Servings: 8

Ingredients:

- *15 oz. beef meat*
- *5 oz. herbs de Provence*
- *2 large onions*
- *2 garlic cloves, chopped*
- *1 cup milk*
- *20 oz. flour*
- *10 oz. rye flour*
- *3 tsp. dry yeast*
- *1 egg*
- *3 tbsp. sunflower oil*
- *1 tbsp. sugar*
- *Sea salt*
- *Ground black pepper*
- *Red pepper*

Directions: Sprinkle the beef meat with the herbs de Provence, salt, black, and red pepper and marinate in milk for overnight. Cube the beef and fry in a skillet or a wok on medium heat until soft (for around 20 minutes).

Chop the onions and garlic. Then fry them until caramelized.

Combine all the ingredients except for the beef and then mix well.

Combine the beef pieces and the dough and mix in the bread machine.

Close the lid and turn the bread machine on the basic program.

Bake the bread until a medium crust and after the bread is ready, take it out and leave for 1 hour covered with the towel; only then can you slice the bread.

Nutrition: Calories 368.4; Carbs 3.4 g; Fat 40.2 g; Protein 28.7 g

Walnut Bread

Preparation Time: 10 minutes
Cooking Time: 4 hours
Servings: 1 1/2 pounds / 10 slices

Ingredients:

- *4 eggs, pasteurized*
- *2 tbsp. apple cider vinegar*
- *4 tbsp. oil*
- *1/2 cup lukewarm water*
- *1 cup walnuts, chopped*
- *1/2 cup flour*
- *1 tbsp. baking powder*
- *2 tbsp. psyllium husk powder*
- *1/2 tsp. salt*

Directions: Take a large bowl, crack eggs, beat in vinegar, oil, and water until blended, and stir in walnuts until just mixed.
Take a separate large bowl, place flour in it, and then stir in baking powder, husk powder, and salt until mixed.
Add egg mixture into the bread bucket, top with flour mixture, shut the lid, select the BASIC/WHITE cycle setting and then press the UP/DOWN arrow button to adjust baking time according to the bread machine; it will take 3–4 hours.
Then press the crust button to select light crust if available, and press the START/STOP button to switch on the bread machine.
When the bread machine beeps, open the lid, take out the bread basket, and lift the bread.
Let bread cool on a wire rack for one hour, then cut it into ten slices and serve.

Nutrition: Calories: 201; Fat: 8.1 g; Carbs: 7.5 g; Fiber: 4.7 g; Protein: 6 g

Almond Butter Bread

Preparation Time: 10 minutes
Cooking Time: 4 hours
Servings: 1 pound / 12 slices

Ingredients:

- *3 eggs, pasteurized*
- *1 cup almond butter*
- *1 tbsp. apple cider vinegar*
- *1/2 tsp. baking soda*

Directions: Crack eggs in a bowl and then beat in butter, vinegar, and baking soda until combined.
Add egg mixture into the bread bucket, shut the lid, select the BASIC/WHITE cycle setting and then press the UP/DOWN arrow button to adjust baking time according to the bread machine; it will take 3–4 hours.
Then press the crust button to select light crust if available, and press the START/STOP button to switch on the bread machine.
When the bread machine beeps, open the lid, take out the bread basket, and lift the bread.
Let bread cool on a wire rack for one hour, then cut it into twelve slices and serve.

Nutrition: Calories: 147.4; Fat: 11.4 g; Carbs: 4.6 g; Fiber: 2.1 g; Protein: 8.4 g

Vegetable Bread

Cauliflower and Garlic Bread

Preparation Time: 10 minutes
Cooking Time: 4 hours
Servings: 9

Ingredients:

- *5 eggs, separated*
- *2/3 cup coconut flour*
- *1 1/2 cup rice cauliflower*
- *1 tsp. garlic, minced*
- *1/2 tsp. sea salt*
- *1/2 tbsp. rosemary, chopped*
- *1/2 tbsp. parsley, chopped*
- *3/4 tbsp. baking powder*
- *3 tbsp. unsalted butter*

Directions: Place the cauliflower rice in a bowl and cover it. Microwave for 3–4 minutes or until steaming. Then drain. Wrap in cheesecloth and remove as much moisture as possible. Set aside.
Place egg whites in a bowl and whisk until stiff peaks form.
Then transfer 1/4 of the whipped egg whites into a food processor. Add remaining ingredients except for cauliflower and pulse for 2 minutes until blended.
Add cauliflower rice, and pulse for 2 minutes until combined. Then pulse in the remaining egg whites until just mixed.
Add batter into the bread bucket and cover. Select the BASIC/WHITE cycle. Press START.
Remove the bread when done. Cool, slice, and serve.

Nutrition: Calories: 105.8; Fat: 6.8 g; Carbs: 2.3 g; Protein: 9.6 g

Vegetable Loaf

Preparation Time: 10 minutes
Cooking Time: 4 hours
Servings: 12 slices

Ingredients:

- *4 eggs*
- *1/4 cup coconut oil*
- *1 medium zucchini, grated*
- *1 cup pumpkin, grated*
- *1 small carrot, grated*
- *1/3 cup coconut flour*
- *1 cup almond flour*
- *2 tbsp. pumpkin seeds*
- *2 tbsp. flaxseeds*
- *2 tbsp. sunflower seeds*
- *2 tbsp. sesame seeds*
- *2 tbsp. psyllium husks*
- *2 tsp. salt*
- *1 tbsp. smoked paprika*
- *2 tsp. cumin, ground*
- *2 tsp. baking powder*

Directions: Beat the eggs until frothy, beat in the oil, and then stir in zucchini, pumpkin, and carrot until just mixed. Place flour in another bowl. Then stir in the remaining ingredients until mixed.
Add egg mixture into the bread bucket, top with flour mixture, and cover.
Select the BASIC/WHITE cycle. Press START. Remove the bread when done. Cool, slice, and serve.

Nutrition: Calories: 178.2; Fat: 12.5 g; Carbs: 5.1 g; Protein: 8.9 g

Almond Pumpkin Bread

Preparation Time: 10 minutes
Cooking Time: 60 minutes
Servings: 16

Ingredients:

- *1/3 cup oil*
- *3 large eggs*
- *1 1/2 cups pumpkin puree, canned*
- *1 cup granulated sugar*
- *1 1/2 tsp. baking powder*
- *1/2 tsp. baking soda*
- *1/4 tsp. salt*
- *3/4 tsp. cinnamon, ground*
- *1/4 tsp. nutmeg, ground*
- *1/4 tsp. ginger, ground*
- *3 cups almond flour*
- *1/2 cup pecans, chopped*

Directions: Grease the bread machine pan with cooking spray. Stir all the wet ingredients in a bowl. Add all the dry ingredients except pecans until mixed.
Pour the batter onto the bread machine pan and place it back inside the bread machine. Close and select QUICK BREAD. Add the pecans after the beep. Remove the bread when done. Cool, slice, and serve.

Nutrition: Calories: 52.4; Fat: 12.3 g; Carbs: 5.3 g; Protein: 11.6 g

Celery Bread

Preparation Time: 10 minutes
Cooking Time: 3 hours
Servings: 1 loaf

Ingredients:

- *1 (10 oz.) can cream of celery soup*
- *3 tbsp. low-fat milk, heated*
- *1 tbsp. vegetable oil*
- *1 1/4 tsp. celery, garlic, or onion salt*
- *3/4 cup celery, fresh, sliced thin*
- *1 tbsp. celery leaves, fresh and chopped*
- *1 egg*
- *3 cups bread flour*
- *1/4 tsp. sugar*
- *1/4 tsp. ginger*
- *1/2 cup quick-cooking oats*
- *2 tbsp. gluten*
- *2 tsp. celery seeds*
- *1 package active dry yeast*

Directions: Add all ingredients to the bread machine. Select the basic bread setting.

Nutrition: Calories 70.2; Fat 2.6 g; Carbs 7.8 g; Protein 4.6 g

Pumpkin and Sunflower Seed Bread

Preparation time: 40 minutes
Cooking time: 40 minutes
Servings: 10

Ingredients:

- *1/2 cup psyllium husk, ground*
- *1/2 cup chia seeds*
- *1/2 cup pumpkin seeds*
- *1/2 cup sunflower seeds*
- *2 tbsp. flaxseed, ground*
- *1 tsp. baking soda*
- *1/4 tsp. salt*
- *3 tbsp. oil*
- *1 1/4 cup egg whites*
- *1/2 cup milk*

Directions: Place all wet ingredients into the bread machine pan first.
Add dry ingredients. Set the bread machine to the gluten-free setting.
When it is done, remove the bread machine pan from the bread machine.
Let cool slightly before transferring to a cooling rack.
You can store the bread for up to 5 days in the refrigerator.

Nutrition: Calories 150.5; Carbs 12.4 g; Fat 7.8 g; Protein 6.5

Keto Onion Bread

Preparation Time: 25 minutes
Cooking Time: 2 hours
Servings: 12

Ingredients:

- *1 1/2 cups water*
- *2 tbsp.+2 tsp. unsalted butter*
- *1 1/2 tsp. salt*
- *1 tbsp.+1 tsp. sugar*
- *2 tbsp.+2 tsp. non-fat dry milk*
- *4 cups almond flour*
- *2 tsp. active dry yeast*
- *4 tbsp. dry onion soup mix*

Directions: Add all ingredients except dry onion soup mix in the bread machine pan.
Close the lid. Select BASIC cycle on the bread machine and then press START.
The machine will ping after around 30–40 minutes.
Pause the bread machine and add the dry onion soup mix.
Press START again and allow the cycle to continue. Once the loaf is finished, transfer it to a cooling rack.
Slice and serve with butter or cream cheese or as a soup side dish.

Nutrition: Calories 326.8; Fat 14.9 g; Carbs 38.8 g; Protein 7.4 g

Sundried Tomato Bread

Preparation Time: 10 minutes
Cooking Time: 2 hours
Servings: 10

Ingredients:

- *2 1/4 cup flour*
- *1 tbsp. baking powder*
- *1 tsp. kosher salt*
- *3 large eggs*
- *1 1/2 cup buttermilk*
- *6 tbsp. canola oil*
- *1 tbsp. basil, dried*
- *1 cup sundried tomato roughly, chopped*

Directions: Place all the fixings in the bread machine bucket except for basil and sundried tomato.
Secure the lid cover. Select the QUICK BREAD setting on the bread machine, then press START.
Wait for the ping, fruit, and nut signal to open the lid, and add the basil and sundried tomato. Place a cover and press START to continue. When the cycle finishes, transfer the loaf to a wire rack and let it cool.
Slice and serve.

Nutrition: Calories 180.2; Fat 4.1 g; Carbs 30.3 g; Protein 3.7 g

Sweet Potato Bread

Preparation Time: 1 hour and 25 minutes
Cooking Time: 12–14 minutes
Servings: 10

Ingredients:

- *1 cup sweet potatoes, cooked and mashed*
- *3 tsp. vanilla extract*
- *1/2 tsp. cloves, ground*
- *1/2 cinnamon*
- *1/2 tsp. nutmeg, ground*
- *1/2 tsp. baking powder*
- *1/4 tsp. baking soda*
- *1/2 tsp. salt*
- *5 eggs*
- *1/2 cup pure maple syrup*
- *1 tsp. of oil*
- *3/4 cup flour*
- *1 1/2 tsp. active dry yeast*

Directions: Get a mixing container and combine the flour, cloves ground, nutmeg ground, cinnamon, baking powder, salt, and baking soda.
Get another mixing container and combine the pure vanilla extract, eggs, maple syrup, mashed fresh sweet potatoes, and oil.
As per the instructions in the machine manual, pour the ingredients into the bread pan, following the yeast instructions.
Put the bread pan in the machine, and select the basic bread setting - together with the bread size and crust type if available - then press start once you have closed the lid of the machine.
When the bread is ready, extract it, and place it on a metallic mesh surface to cool completely before cutting and.

Nutrition: Calories 91, Fat 1.59 g, Carbs 17.72 g, Protein 1.74 g

Onion Bread

Preparation Time: 20 minutes
Cooking Time: 5 minutes
Servings: 6

Ingredients:

- *1 red onion, diced and sautéed with 1/2 tsp. butter until golden brown*
- *3 tsp. unsalted butter, melted*
- *1/4 tsp. salt*
- *1/4 tsp. garlic, ground*
- *3 tsp. psyllium husk flour*
- *5 eggs*
- *1/2 tsp. baking powder*
- *3/4 tsp. active dry yeast*
- *1/2 tsp. onion powder*
- *1 cup flour*

Directions: Get a mixing container and combine the flour, salt, psyllium husk flour, ground onion, baking powder, and ground garlic.
Get another mixing container and mix the melted unsalted butter, eggs, and sautéed onions.

As per the instructions in the machine manual, pour the ingredients into the bread pan and follow the yeast instructions.
Put the bread pan into the machine, and select the basic bread setting - together with the bread size and crust type if available - then press start once you have closed the lid of the machine.
When the bread is ready, extract it, and place it on a metallic mesh surface to cool completely before cutting and eating it.

Nutrition: Calories 124.7; Fat 9.2 g; Carbs 1.3g; Protein 9.4g

Beetroot Bread

Preparation Time: 30 minutes
Cooking Time: 45 minutes
Servings: 2

Ingredients:

- *1 cup fresh beetroot, grated*
- *1 cup almond flour*
- *1/2 cup coconut flour*
- *1/2 tsp. nutmeg, ground*
- *1/4 tsp. cinnamon, ground*
- *2 tsp. active dry yeast*
- *1/3 cup Swerve sweetener*
- *1/2 cup warm water*
- *4 tsp. unsalted butter, melted*
- *1/3 cup walnuts, roasted and sliced*
- *1 tsp. baking powder*
- *1/4 tsp. salt*

Directions: Get a mixing container and combine the almond flour, coconut flour, roasted walnuts, Swerve sweetener, cinnamon ground, nutmeg powder, and baking powder.
Get another container and combine the warm water, shredded beetroot, and melted unsalted butter.
As per the instructions in the machine manual, pour the ingredients in the bread pan, taking care to follow how to mix in the yeast.
In the machine, place the bread pan, select the sweet bread setting - together with the crust type if available - then press start once you have closed the lid of the machine.
When the bread is ready, remove the bread pan from the machine using oven mitts. Use a stainless spatula to extract the bread from the pan and turn the pan upside down on a metallic rack where the bread will cool off before slicing it.

Nutrition: Calories 852.4; Fat 41.4 g; Carbs 100.3 g; Protein 23.4 g

Tomato Bread

Preparation Time: 15 minutes
Cooking Time: 45 minutes
Servings: 1.5 lb./16 Slices

Ingredients:

- *4 whole eggs*
- *2 tbsp. salted butter, melted*
- *1 cup flaxseed meal*
- *4 tsp. oat fiber*
- *2 tsp. baking powder*
- *1/4 tsp. sea salt*
- *1/2 tsp. basil, dried*
- *1/4 tsp. garlic powder*
- *2 tbsp. sun-dried tomatoes, diced*
- *1/4 cup parmesan, grated*

Directions: Carefully whisk eggs and butter together. Pour all the ingredients into the bread machine pan. Close the lid. Set the bread machine program to CAKE for 30–45 minutes (depending on the bread machine model) and choose the crust color LIGHT. Press START. Help the bread machine knead the dough with a spatula, if necessary. Before the baking mode begins, sprinkle the top with grated parmesan.
After baking for 20 minutes, check for doneness with a toothpick. Wait until the program is complete, then take the bucket out and let it cool for 5–10 minutes.
Shake the loaf from the pan and let it cool for 30 minutes on a cooling rack.
Slice and serve.

Nutrition: Calories 87.8; Carbs 2.2 g; Fat 5.1 g

Zucchini Lemon Bread

Preparation Time: 5 minutes
Cooking Time: 40 minutes
Servings: 12

Ingredients:

- *2 cups flour*
- *3/4 tsp. salt*
- *1 tsp. baking powder*
- *1/2 tsp. baking soda*
- *2 cups zucchini, grated*
- *2 tsp. vanilla extract*
- *1/3 cup sugar*
- *2 lemons zest*
- *3 eggs*
- *3/4 cup unsalted butter, melted*
- *2 tsp. lemon juice, fresh*
- *1 1/2 tsp. active dry yeast*

Directions: In a mixing container, combine the flour, salt, baking powder, and baking soda.
Get another mixing bowl and combine the shredded zucchini, pure vanilla extract, sugar, lemon zest, lemon juice, eggs, and unsalted melted butter.
As per the instructions in the manual of the machine, pour the ingredients into the bread pan, taking care to follow how to mix in the yeast.
In the machine, place the bread pan, and select the basic bread setting - together with the bread size and crust type, if available - then press start once you have closed the lid of the machine.
When the bread is ready, remove the bread pan from the machine using oven mitts. Use a stainless spatula to extract the bread from the pan and turn the pan upside down on a metallic rack where the bread will cool off before slicing it.

Nutrition: Calories 228.7; Fat 15.7g; Carbs 14.2 g; Protein 3.5 g

Carrot Bread

Preparation Time: 2h 10 Mins
Servings: 1 loaf / 8 slices

Ingredients:

- *4 eggs*
- *¼ teaspoon kosher salt*
- *½ cup (4 oz) butter*
- *½ cup (4 oz) sugar*
- *1 tablespoon vanilla sugar*
- *2 teaspoon cinnamon*
- *3 cups (13.50 oz) all-purpose flour*
- *1 tablespoon baking powder*
- *¼ cup ground nuts*
- *¾ cup carrot, grated*

Directions: Follow the manufacturer's instructions and put all the ingredients into the bread machine (except the carrot). Set the program of the bread machine to CAKE/SWEET and set the crust type to LIGHT.

Press START. Once the machine beeps, add a grated carrot. When the cycle is completed, take the bucket out and let the loaf cool for 5 minutes.

Shake the bucket gently to remove the loaf, then transfer to a cooling rack, slice, and serve. Enjoy!

Nutrition: Calories 395.8; Fat 15.7 g; Carbs 52.3 g; Protein 10.2 g

Zucchini Bread

Preparation Time: 2h 10 Mins
Servings: 1 loaf / 8 slices

Ingredients:

- *2 eggs*
- *¼ teaspoon salt*
- *1 cup oil*
- *1 cup white sugar*
- *1 tablespoon vanilla sugar*
- *2 teaspoon cinnamon*
- *½ cup nuts, ground*
- *3 cups all-purpose flour, well sifted*
- *1 tablespoon baking powder*
- *1¼ cup zucchini, grated*

Directions: Follow the manufacturer's instructions and put all the ingredients into the bread machine (except the zucchini).

Set the program of the bread machine to CAKE/SWEET and set the crust type to LIGHT.

Press START. Once the machine beeps, add zucchini. When the cycle is completed, take the bucket out and let the loaf cool for 5 minutes.

Shake the bucket gently to remove the loaf, then transfer to a cooling rack, slice, and serve.

Nutrition: Calories 555.6; Fat 30.1g; Carbs 62.3 g; Protein 9.6 g

Pumpkin Bread

Preparation Time: 10 minutes
Cooking Time: 4 hours
Servings: 1 1/2 pound / 12 slices

Ingredients:

- *2 eggs, pasteurized*
- *1 cup butter*
- *2/3 cup sugar*
- *2/3 cup pumpkin puree*
- *1/8 tsp. cloves, ground*
- *1/2 tsp. cinnamon, ground*
- *1/8 tsp. ginger, ground*
- *1 tsp. baking powder*
- *1/2 tsp. nutmeg, ground*

Directions: Take a large bowl, crack eggs, and then beat the remaining ingredients in the order described in the ingredients until incorporated.
Add batter into the bread bucket, shut the lid, select the basic/white cycle setting and then press the UP/DOWN arrow button to adjust baking time according to the bread machine; it will take 3–4 hours.
Then press the crust button to select light crust if available, and press the START/STOP button to switch on the bread machine.
When the bread machine beeps, open the lid, take out the bread basket, and lift the bread.
Let bread cool on a wire rack for one hour, then cut it into 12 slices and serve.

Nutrition: Calories: 148.2; Fat: 12.9 g ; Carbs: 7 g ; Fiber: 2 g; Protein: 6.7 g

Sweet Bread

Lemon Poppy Seed Bread

Preparation Time: 10 minutes
Cooking Time: 4 hours
Servings: 6

Ingredients:

- *3 eggs*
- *1 1/2 tbsp. unsalted butter, melted*
- *1 1/2 tbsp. lemon juice*
- *1 lemon, zested*
- *1 1/2 cups flour*
- *1/4 cup granulated sugar*
- *1/4 tsp. baking powder*
- *1 tbsp. poppy seeds*

Directions: Beat eggs, butter, lemon juice, and lemon zest until combined.
Add flour, sugar, baking powder, and poppy seeds in another bowl and mix well.
Add the egg mixture to the bread pan, top with the flour mixture, and cover.
Select the BASIC/WHITE cycle and press START.
Remove the bread when done. Cool, slice, and serve.

Nutrition: Calories: 200.1; Fat: 15.5 g; Carbs: 2.4 g; Protein: 9.2 g

Cinnamon Sweet Bread

Preparation Time: 10 minutes
Cooking Time: 1 hour
Servings: 12

Ingredients:

- *3 tsp. cinnamon, ground*
- *1 1/2 cups almond flour*
- *3 large eggs*
- *1/2 cup keto sweetener*
- *1 tsp. vanilla essence*
- *1/4 cup coconut flour*
- *1/4 cup sour cream*
- *1 tsp. baking powder*
- *1/2 cup almond milk, unsweetened*
- *1/2 cup unsalted butter, melted*

Directions: Put all ingredients into the bread machine.
Close the lid and choose the sweet bread mode.
When cooking is over, remove the bread from the machine and let it rest for about 10 minutes.

Nutrition: Calories 190.1; Fat 15.7 g; Carbs 4.5 g; Protein 7.5 g

Cranberry Bread

Preparation Time: 10 minutes
Cooking Time: 3 hours 18 minutes
Servings: 12

Ingredients:

- *2 1/2 cups flour*
- *2 tsp. baking powder*
- *2 cups fresh cranberries*
- *1 tbsp. orange zest*
- *1 cup erythritol or stevia*
- *1/2 tsp. salt*
- *8 eggs*
- *8 oz. cream cheese*
- *2 tsp. orange extract*
- *1/2 cup unsalted butter*

Directions: Put all ingredients into the bread machine. Close the lid and choose the sweet bread mode. When the cooking time is over, remove the bread from the machine and let it rest for about 10 minutes.

Nutrition: Calories 335.7; Fat 30.1 g; Carbs 5.7 g; Protein 10.7 g

Bread Rolls

Preparation Time: 10 minutes
Cooking Time: 15 minutes + dough preparation
Servings: 8

Ingredients:

- *2 cups flour*
- *3 tbsp. psyllium husk powder*
- *2 tsp. baking powder*
- *3 tbsp. whey protein powder*
- *2 tsp. insulin*
- *2 tsp. active dry yeast*
- *2 egg whites*
- *2 eggs*
- *1/4 cup butter*
- *1/3 cup lukewarm water*
- *1/4 cup Greek yogurt*

Directions: Put all ingredients to the bread machine.
Select dough setting. When the time is over, transfer the dough to the floured surface. Shape it into a ball and cut it into about 8 pieces. Line a pie dish with parchment paper. Form 8 dough balls. Cover the dish with greased cling film and sit for 60 minutes in a warm place. Prepare the oven to 350°F and bake for 15 minutes. Cover with foil and bake for 10 more minutes.

Nutrition: Calories 255.7; Fat 18.1 g; Carbs 5.1 g; Protein 14.4 g

Basic Sweet Yeast Bread

Preparation Time: 3 hours
Cooking Time: 20 minutes
Servings: 8

Ingredients:

- *1 egg*
- *1/4 cup butter*
- *1/3 cup sugar*
- *1 cup milk*
- *1/2 tsp. salt*
- *4 cups flour*
- *1 tbsp. active dry yeast*

After beeping:

- *Fruits/groundnuts*

Directions:
Put all ingredients into the bread machine, carefully following the instructions of the manufacturer (except fruits/groundnuts).
Set the program of the bread machine to basic/sweet and set the crust type to light or medium.
Press start. Once the machine beeps, add fruits/ground nuts.
When the cycle is completed, take the bucket out and let the loaf cool for 5 minutes.
Shake the bucket gently to remove the loaf, then transfer to a cooling rack, slice, and serve.

Nutrition: Calorie 336.4; Carbs 2.4 g; Fat 7.2 g; Protein 9.8 g

Apricot Prune Bread

Preparation Time: 3 hours
Cooking Time: 20 minutes
Servings: 8

Ingredients:

- *1 egg*
- *4/5 cup whole milk*
- *1/4 cup apricot juice*
- *1/4 cup butter*
- *1/5 cup sugar*
- *4 cups flour*
- *1 tbsp. instant yeast*
- *1/4 tsp. salt*
- *5/8 cup prunes, chopped*
- *5/8 cup dried apricots, chopped*

Directions: Put all ingredients into the bread machine, carefully following the manufacturer's instructions (except apricots and prunes).
Set the program of the bread machine to basic/sweet and set the crust type to light or medium.
Press start. Once the machine beeps, add apricots and prunes.
When the cycle is completed, take the bucket out and let the loaf cool for 5 minutes.
Shake the bucket gently to remove the loaf, then transfer to a cooling rack, slice, and serve.

Nutrition: Calories 362.5; Carbs 2.4 g; Fat 6.2 g; Protein 11.9 g

Citrus Bread

Preparation Time: 3 hours
Cooking Time: 1 hour
Servings: 8

Ingredients:

- *1 egg*
- *3 tbsp. butter*
- *1/3 cup sugar*
- *1 tbsp. vanilla sugar*
- *1/2 cup orange juice*
- *2/3 cup milk*
- *1 tsp. salt*
- *4 cup almond flour*
- *1 tbsp. instant yeast*
- *1/4 cup oranges, candied*
- *1/4 cup lemon, candied*
- *2 tsp. lemon zest*
- *1/4 cup almonds, chopped*

Directions: Put all ingredients into the bread machine, carefully following the instructions of the manufacturer (except candied fruits, zest, and almonds).
Set the program of the bread machine to basic/sweet and set the crust type to light or medium.
Press start. Once the machine beeps, add candied fruits, lemon zest, and chopped almonds.
When the cycle is completed, take the bucket out and let the loaf cool for 5 minutes.
Shake the bucket gently to remove the loaf, then transfer to a cooling rack, slice, and serve.

Nutrition: Calories 402.4; Carbs 3.4 g; Fat 7.1 g; Protein 12.8 g

Fruit Bread

Preparation Time: 3 hours
Cooking Time: 40 minutes
Servings: 8

Ingredients:

- *1 egg*
- *1 cup milk*
- *2 tbsp. rum*
- *1/4 cup butter*
- *1/4 cup brown sugar*
- *4 cups almond flour*
- *1 tbsp. instant yeast*
- *1 tsp. salt*

Fruits:

- *1/4 cups dried apricots, coarsely chopped*
- *1/4 cups prunes, coarsely chopped*
- *1/4 cups candied cherry, pitted*
- *1/2 cup seedless raisins*
- *1/4 cup almonds, chopped*

Directions: Put all ingredients into the bread machine, carefully following the instructions of the manufacturer (except fruits). Set the program of the bread machine to basic/sweet and set crust type to light or medium. Press start. Once the machine beeps, add fruits. When the cycle is completed, take the bucket out and let the loaf cool for 5 minutes.
Shake the bucket gently to remove the loaf, then transfer to a cooling rack, slice, and serve.

Nutrition: Calories 440.4; Carbs 3.5 g; Fat 9.7 g; Protein 12.8 g

Marzipan Cherry Bread

Preparation Time: 3 hours
Cooking Time: 35 minutes
Servings: 8

Ingredients:

- *1 egg*
- *3/4 cup milk*
- *1 tbsp. almond liqueur*
- *4 tbsp. orange juice*
- *1/2 cup ground almonds*
- *1/4 cup butter*
- *1/3 cup sugar*
- *4 cups flour*
- *1 tbsp. instant yeast*
- *1 tsp. salt*
- *1/2 cup marzipan*
- *1/2 cup dried cherries, pitted*

Directions: Put all ingredients into the bread machine, carefully following the instructions of the manufacturer (except marzipan and cherry).
Set the program of the bread machine to basic/sweet and set the crust type to light or medium.
Press start.
Once the machine beeps, add marzipan and cherry. When the cycle is completed, take the bucket out and let the loaf cool for 5 minutes.
Shake the bucket gently to remove the loaf, then transfer to a cooling rack, slice, and serve.

Nutrition: Calories 508.1; Carbs 3.1 g; Fat 14.4 g; Protein 18.2 g

Raspberry Bread

Preparation Time: 10 minutes
Cooking Time: 50 minutes
Servings: 12 slices

Ingredients:

- *1 cup raspberries*
- *1/4 cup sugar*
- *1 1/2 tsp. baking powder*
- *2 cups flour*
- *4 tbsp. sour cream*
- *4 tbsp. unsalted butter, melted*
- *2 whole eggs*
- *1 tsp. vanilla*
- *1 tsp. lemon extract*
- *1/2 lemon, juiced*

Directions: Put all the ingredients (except the raspberries) to the bread machine pan following the instructions for the device. Close the cover. Set the bread machine program to CAKE for 40–50 minutes.
After the signal, add the raspberries to the dough. Press START.
Check for doneness with a toothpick. The approximate baking time is 45 minutes.
Wait until the program is complete. When done, take the bucket out and let it cool for 10 minutes.
Shake the loaf from the pan and let it cool for 30 minutes on a cooling rack.
Slice and serve.

Nutrition: Calories: 165.8; Carbs: 7.3 g; Fat: 12.8 g

Blueberry Bread

Preparation Time: 10 minutes
Cooking Time: 50 minutes
Servings: 12 slices

Ingredients:

- *1/2 cup blueberries*
- *1/3 cup sugar*
- *2 tsp. baking powder*
- *2 cups flour*
- *4 tbsp. sour cream*
- *4 tbsp. unsalted butter, melted*
- *2 whole eggs*
- *1 tsp. vanilla*

Directions: In a large bowl, beat eggs with an electric mixer well.
Pour them into the bread machine pan. Add all other ingredients. Close the lid.
Set the bread machine program to CAKE for 45–60 minutes (depending on the device).
Press START. After the signal indicating the beginning of the BAKE mode, add the blueberries.
After 35 minutes of baking, start checking for doneness using a toothpick. The approximate baking time is 45–50 minutes. Wait until the program is complete. When done, take the bucket out and let it cool for 10 minutes.
Shake the loaf from the pan and let it cool for 30 minutes on a cooling rack.
Slice and serve.

Nutrition: Calories: 163.5; Carbs: 10.2 g; Fat: 11.5 g

Banana Bread

Preparation Time: 10 minutes
Cooking Time: 60–70 minutes
Servings: 16 slices

Ingredients:

- *2 1/2 cup flour*
- *1 cup mashed banana (2 large bananas)*
- *6 large eggs, beaten*
- *4 tbsp. ghee, melted*
- *1/2 cup sugar*
- *2 tbsp. cinnamon*
- *1 tbsp. baking powder*
- *1/2 cup walnuts, crushed*
- *1/4 tsp. ground nutmeg*

Directions: In a large bowl, combine all of the dry ingredients. In a small bowl, beat the eggs with an electric mixer.
Pour eggs and all of the wet ingredients into the bread machine pan.
Cover them with dry ingredients. Close the lid.
Set the bread machine program to DOUGH. The time may vary depending on the device. Press START.
After the program completes, start the Bake mode for 55 minutes. After 45 minutes of baking, start checking for doneness using a toothpick. The approximate baking time is 45–60 minutes. Wait until the program is complete. When done, take the bucket out and let it cool for 10 minutes. Shake the loaf from the pan and let it cool for 30 minutes on a cooling rack.
Slice and serve.

Nutrition: Calories: 187.1; Carbs: 8.9 g; Fat 12.2 g; Cholesterol 72.8 g; Sodium 170.3 mg

Avocado Bread

Preparation Time: 10 minutes
Cooking Time: 60–70 minutes
Servings: 14 slices

Ingredients:

- *4 avocados, mashed*
- *2 cups almond flour*
- *1 cup coconut flour*
- *1/2 cup monk fruit sweetener*
- *5 tbsp. avocado oil*
- *4 tbsp. cocoa powder, unsweetened*
- *1/2 tsp. kosher salt*
- *1 tsp. baking soda*
- *1 tsp. vanilla extract*
- *1 cup chocolate chips*

Directions: In a large bowl, combine all of the dry ingredients.
In a blender, combine all of the wet ingredients.
Put all of the wet ingredients into the bread machine pan.
Cover them with dry ingredients. Add half of the chocolate chips.
Close the cover. Set the bread machine program to CAKE. The time may vary depending on the device.
Press START. Help the machine to knead the dough, if necessary.
Before baking, top the bread with the remaining 1/2 cup of chocolate chips.
After 45 minutes of baking, start checking for doneness using a toothpick. The approximate baking time is 45–60 minutes. Wait until the program is complete.
When done, take the bucket out and let it cool for 10 minutes.
Shake the loaf from the pan and let it cool for 30 minutes on a cooling rack.
Slice and serve.

Nutrition: Calories: 287.5; Carbs: 15.5 g; Fat 22.1 g

Gingerbread Cake

Preparation Time: 10 minutes
Cooking Time: 45 minutes
Servings: 10 slices

Ingredients:

- *4 large eggs*
- *1/4 cup butter, melted*
- *1 tsp. vanilla extract*
- *3/4 cup (3 oz.) granulated sugar*
- *3/4 cup (5 oz.) flour*
- *1 tsp. baking powder*
- *2 tsp. ginger, ground*
- *2 tsp. cinnamon, ground*
- *1/2 tsp. allspice, ground*
- *1/2 tsp. nutmeg, ground*
- *1/2 tsp. clove, ground*
- *1/4 tsp. kosher salt*

For the icing:

- *1/2 cup (1.2 oz.) cream cheese, softened*
- *1/4 cup (1.4 oz.) sugar*
- *1 tsp. vanilla extract*
- *1/4 cup walnuts, chopped*

Directions: Whisk together the eggs, vanilla, and unsalted butter.
In a bowl, mix all the dry ingredients. Put all of the wet ingredients into the bread machine pan.
Cover them with dry ingredients. Close the lid.
Set the bread machine program to CAKE. The time may vary depending on the device.
Press START. After 30 minutes of baking, start checking for doneness using a toothpick. The approximate baking time is 40–45 minutes. Wait until the program is complete. When done, take the bucket out and let it cool for 10 minutes.
Shake the loaf from the pan and let it cool for 30 minutes on a cooling rack.
Slice and serve.

Nutrition: Calories: 138.4; Carbs: 12.3 g; Fat: 11.3 g

Lemon Bread

Cooking Time: 1 hour
Servings: 12 slices

Ingredients:

- *9.5 oz. flour*
- *1/2 tsp. baking powder*
- *1/2 cup sugar*
- *2 tbsp. poppy seeds*
- *2 lemons zest*
- *2 tbsp. lemon juice*
- *3 tbsp. butter, melted*
- *6 whole eggs*

For the Icing:

- *1/2 cup sugar*
- *1 tbsp. lemon juice*
- *2 tbsp. water*

Directions: Put all ingredients into the bread machine pan. Close the lid.
Set the bread machine program to CAKE. The time may vary depending on the device.
Press START. Help the machine to knead the dough, if necessary.
After 40 minutes of baking, start checking for doneness using a toothpick. The approximate baking time is 45–55 minutes.
Wait until the program is complete, and when done, take the bucket out and let it cool for 10 minutes.
Shake the loaf from the pan and let it cool for 30 minutes on a cooling rack.
Make the icing in a small bowl, mixing all the ingredients. Drizzle it over the bread.
Slice and serve.

Nutrition: Calories: 191.2; Carbs: 14.9 g; Fat: 15.7 g

Holiday Bread

Preparation Time: 30 minutes
Cooking Time: 30-40 minutes
Servings: 2 pounds / 12 slices

Ingredients:

- *2 1/2 cups flour*
- *2 cups whey isolate*
- *1 cup lukewarm water*
- *1/4 cup milk*
- *1/2 cup sugar*
- *1/2 cup butter, melted*
- *1 1/2 tbsp. baking powder*
- *1/2 tsp. sea salt*

For the icing:

- *1/2 cup sugar*
- *1 tbsp. lemon juice*
- *2 Tbsp. water*

Directions: Put all ingredients into the bread machine pan. Close the lid.
Set the bread machine program to CAKE. The time may vary depending on the device.
Press START. Help the machine to knead the dough, if necessary.
After 25 minutes of baking, start checking for doneness using a toothpick. The approximate baking time is 30–35 minutes. Wait until the program is complete, and when done, take the bucket out and let it cool for 10 minutes.
Shake the loaf from the pan and let it cool for 30 minutes on a cooling rack.
Make the icing in a small bowl, mixing all the ingredients. Drizzle it over the bread.
Slice and serve.

Nutrition: Calories: 125.8; Carbs: 10.2 g; Fat: 11.5 g

Cinnamon Bread

Preparation Time: 10 minutes
Cooking Time: 4 hours
Servings: 2 pounds / 10 slices

Ingredients:

- *3 tbsp. sour cream*
- *3 eggs, pasteurized*
- *2 tsp. vanilla extract, unsweetened*
- *1/4 cup unsalted butter, melted*
- *2 cups flour*
- *1/3 cup sugar*
- *2 tbsp. cinnamon*
- *1 tsp. baking soda*
- *1 tsp. baking powder*

Directions: Take a large bowl, place sour cream in it and then beat in eggs, vanilla, and butter until combined.
Take a separate large bowl, place flour in it, and then stir in sugar, cinnamon, baking powder, and soda until mixed.
Add egg mixture into the bread bucket, top with flour mixture, shut the lid, select the BASIC/WHITE cycle setting and then press the UP/DOWN arrow button to adjust baking time according to the bread machine; it will take 3–4 hours.
Then press the crust button to select light crust if available, and press the START/STOP button to switch on the bread machine.
When the bread machine beeps, open the lid, take out the bread basket, and lift the bread.
Let bread cool on a wire rack for one hour, then cut it into ten slices and serve.

Nutrition: Calories: 163.4; Fat: 11.5 g; Carbs: 3.2 g; Fiber: 1.2 g; Protein: 6.4 g

Lemon Raspberry Loaf

Preparation Time: 10 minutes
Cooking Time: 4 hours
Servings: 2 pounds / 12 slices

Ingredients:

- *2 eggs, pasteurized*
- *4 tbsp. sour cream*
- *1 tsp. vanilla extract, unsweetened*
- *1 tsp. lemon extract, unsweetened*
- *4 tbsp. unsalted butter, melted*
- *1/4 cup sugar*
- *2 tbsp. lemon juice*
- *1/2 cup raspberries preserves*
- *2 cups flour*
- *1 1/2 tsp. baking powder*

Directions: Take a large bowl, place flour in it, and then stir in baking soda until mixed.
Take a separate large bowl, crack eggs in it, beat in sour cream, extracts, butter, sugar, and lemon juice until blended, and then stir in raspberry preserve until just combined.
Add egg mixture into the bread bucket, top with flour mixture, shut the lid, select the BASIC/WHITE cycle setting and then press the UP/DOWN arrow button to adjust baking time according to the bread machine; it will take 3–4 hours. Then press the crust button to select light crust if available, and press the START/STOP button to switch on the bread machine. When the bread machine beeps, open the lid, take out the bread basket, and lift the bread. Let bread cool on a wire rack for one hour, then cut it into twelve slices and serve.

Nutrition: Calories: 168.2; Fat: 12.3 g; Carbs: 4.5 g; Fiber: 2.1 g; Protein: 5.6 g

Chocolate Zucchini Bread

Preparation Time: 10 minutes
Cooking Time: 4 hours
Servings: 2 pounds / 14 slices

Ingredients:

- *1 cup zucchini, grated, moisture squeezed thoroughly*
- *1/3 cup ground flaxseed*
- *1/2 cup almond flour*
- *1/2 tsp. salt*
- *2 1/2 tsp. baking powder*
- *1 1/4 tbsp. psyllium husk powder*
- *1/3 cup cocoa powder*
- *4 eggs, pasteurized*
- *1 tbsp. coconut cream*
- *5 tbsp. coconut oil*
- *3/4 cup sugar*
- *1 tsp. vanilla extract,*
- *1/2 cup sour cream*
- *1/2 cup chocolate chips, unsweetened*

Directions: Wrap zucchini in cheesecloth and twist well until all the moisture is released. Set aside until required.
Take a large bowl, place flaxseed and flour, and then stir salt, baking powder, husk, and cocoa powder until mixed.
Take a separate large bowl, crack eggs and then beat in coconut cream, coconut oil, sugar, and vanilla until combined.
Blend in half of the flour mixture, then sour cream and the remaining half of the flour mixture until incorporated, and fold in chocolate chips until mixed.
Add batter into the bread bucket, shut the lid, select the BASIC/WHITE cycle setting and then press the UP/DOWN arrow button to adjust baking time according to the bread machine; it will take 3–4 hours.
Then press the crust button to select light crust if available, and press the START/STOP button to switch on the bread machine.
When the bread machine beeps, open the lid, take out the bread basket, and lift the bread.
Let bread cool on a wire rack for one hour, then cut it into fourteen slices and serve.

Nutrition: Calories: 184.2; Fat: 15.9 g; Carbs: 8.8 g; Fiber: 5.2 g; Protein: 6.2 g

Strawberry Bread

Preparation Time: 10 minutes
Cooking Time: 4 hours
Servings: 2 pounds / 10 slices

Ingredients:

- *5 eggs, pasteurized*
- *1 egg white, pasteurized*
- *1 1/2 tsp. vanilla extract*
- *2 tbsp. heavy whipping cream*
- *2 tbsp. sour cream*
- *1 cup monk fruit powder*
- *1 1/2 tsp. baking powder*
- *1/2 tsp. salt*
- *1/2 tsp. cinnamon*
- *8 tbsp. butter, melted*
- *3/4 cup flour*
- *3/4 cup strawberries, chopped*

Directions: Take a large bowl, crack eggs and then beat in egg white, vanilla, heavy cream, sour cream, baking powder, salt, and cinnamon until well combined.
Then stir in flour and fold in strawberries until mixed.

Add batter into the bread bucket, shut the lid, select the BASIC/WHITE cycle or LOW-CARBS setting and then press the UP/DOWN arrow button to adjust baking time according to the bread machine; it will take 3–4 hours.
Then press the crust button to select light crust if available, and press the START/STOP button to switch on the bread machine.
When the bread machine beeps, open the lid, take out the bread basket, and lift the bread.
Let bread cool on a wire rack for one hour, then cut it into ten slices and serve.

Nutrition: Calories: 200.2; Fat: 14.4 g; Carbs: 4.1 g; Fiber: 2.3 g; Protein: 5.7 g

Cranberry and Orange Bread

Preparation Time: 10 minutes
Cooking Time: 4 hours
Servings: 1 1/2 pound / 12 slices

Ingredients:

- *1 cup cranberries, chopped*
- *2/3 cup+3 tbsp. monk fruit powder, divided*
- *5 eggs, pasteurized*
- *1 egg white, pasteurized*
- *2 tbsp. sour cream*
- *1 1/2 tsp. orange extract,*
- *1 tsp. vanilla extract,*
- *9 tbsp. unsalted butter, melted*
- *9 tbsp. flour*
- *1 1/2 tsp. baking powder*
- *1/4 tsp. salt*

Directions: Take a small bowl, place cranberries, and then stir in 4 tbsp. of monk fruit powder until combined. Set aside until required.
Take a large bowl, crack eggs in it, beat in remaining ingredients in it in the order described in the ingredients until incorporated, and then fold in cranberries until just mixed.
Add batter into the bread bucket, shut the lid, select the BASIC/WHITE cycle or LOW-CARBS setting and then press the UP/DOWN arrow button to adjust baking time according to the bread machine; it will take 3–4 hours.
Then press the crust button to select light crust if available, and press the START/STOP button to switch on the bread machine.
When the bread machine beeps, open the lid, take out the bread basket, and lift the bread.
Let bread cool on a wire rack for one hour, then cut it into twelve slices and serve.

Nutrition: Calories: 141.3; Fat: 12.1 g; Carbs: 2.4 g; Fiber: 1.2 g; Protein: 5.9 g

Sweet Avocado Bread

Preparation Time: 10 minutes
Cooking Time: 4 hours
Servings: 1 1/2 pounds / 12 slices

Ingredients:

- *3 eggs, pasteurized*
- *2 tbsp. sugar*
- *1 tbsp. vanilla extract*
- *1 1/2 cups avocado, mashed and ripe*
- *6 tbsp. flour*
- *3/4 tsp. baking soda*
- *1/2 tsp. salt*
- *2 tbsp. cocoa powder, unsweetened*

Directions: Take a large bowl, crack eggs, beat in sweetener and vanilla until fluffy, and then mix in avocado.
Take a separate large bowl, place flour, and then stir in the remaining ingredients until mixed.
Add egg mixture into the bread bucket, top with flour mixture, shut the lid, select the BASIC/WHITE cycle or LOW-CARBS setting, and then press the UP/DOWN arrow button to adjust baking time according to the bread machine; it will take 3–4 hours. Then press the crust button to select light crust if available, and press the START/STOP button to switch on the bread machine.
When the bread machine beeps, open the lid, take out the bread basket, and lift the bread.
Let bread cool on a wire rack for 1 hour, then cut it into twelve slices and serve.

Nutrition: Calories 91.3; Fat: 4.1 g; Carbs: 2.2 g; Fiber: 2.5 g; Protein: 8.2 g

Raisin Bread

Preparation Time: 3 hour
Servings: 1 loaf / 8 slices

Ingredients:

- *1 egg*
- *1 cup (8 oz) milk*
- *¼ cup (2 oz) butter*
- *¼ cup (1.78 oz) sugar*
- *4 cups (18 oz) all-purpose flour/bread flour*
- *1 tablespoon instant yeast*
- *1 teaspoon salt*
- *½ cup (6 oz) raisins*

Directions: Follow the manufacturer's instructions carefully and put all the ingredients into the bread machine (except raisins). Set the program of the bread machine to BASIC/SWEET and set the crust type to LIGHT or MEDIUM. Press START. Once the machine beeps, add raisins. When the cycle is completed, take the bucket out and let the loaf cool for 5 minutes.
Shake the bucket gently to remove the loaf, then transfer to a cooling rack, slice, and serve.

Nutrition: Calories 367.8; Fat 5.7 g; Carbs 65.6 g; Protein 11.2 g

Honey Almond Bread

Preparation Time: 3 hour
Servings: 1 loaf / 8 slices

Ingredients:

- *2 eggs*
- *1 cup milk*
- *¼ cup butter*
- *2 tablespoons sugar*
- *1 tablespoon honey*
- *4 cups all-purpose flour/bread flour*
- *1 tablespoon instant yeast*
- *1 teaspoon salt*

After beeping:

- *¼ cup almonds, chopped*
- *½ cup ground almonds*

Directions: Follow the manufacturer's instructions carefully and put all the ingredients into the bread machine (except almonds).
Set the program of the bread machine to BASIC/SWEET and set the crust type to LIGHT or MEDIUM.
Press START. Once the machine beeps, add almonds. When the cycle is completed, take the bucket out and let the loaf cool for 5 minutes.
Shake the bucket gently to remove the loaf, then transfer to a cooling rack, slice, and serve.

Nutrition: Calories 430.1; Fat 14.3 g; Carbs 57.9 g; Protein 14.3 g

Orange Bread

Preparation Time: 2h 10 Mins
Servings: 1 loaf / 8 slices

Ingredients:

- *4 eggs*
- *4 tablespoons orange juice*
- *½ cup butter*
- *½ cup sugar*
- *1 tablespoon vanilla sugar*
- *2 ½ cups all-purpose flour*
- *1 tablespoon baking powder*
- *¼ cup starch*
- *2 tablespoons orange zest*
- *2 tablespoons candied oranges*

Directions: Follow the manufacturer's instructions carefully and put all the ingredients into the bread machine (except the orange zest and candied oranges).
Set the program of the bread machine to CAKE/SWEET and set the crust type to LIGHT.
Press START. Once the machine beeps, add orange zest and candied oranges.
When the cycle is completed, take the bucket out and let the loaf cool for 5 minutes.
Shake the bucket gently to remove the loaf, then transfer to a cooling rack, slice, and serve.

Nutrition: Calories 370.2; Fat 1 g; Carbs 54.5 g; Protein 8.7 g

Light Cornbread

Preparation Time: 15 minutes
Cooking Time: 40 minutes
Servings: 8

Ingredients:

- *4 eggs*
- *1 1/2 cup almond flour*
- *1/2 cup Swerve sweetener*
- *1 tsp. vanilla extract*
- *1 tsp. baking powder*
- *4 tsp. unsalted butter, melted*

Directions: In a mixing container, combine the almond flour, Swerve sweetener, and baking powder. In another mixing container, combine the eggs, pure vanilla extract, and unsalted melted butter.
As per the instructions in the manual of the machine, pour the ingredients into the bread pan, taking care to follow how to mix in the yeast.
In the machine, place the bread pan, and select the basic bread setting - together with the bread size and crust type, if available - then press start once you have closed the lid of the machine.
When the bread is ready, remove the bread pan from the machine using oven mitts. Use a stainless spatula to extract the bread from the pan, and turn the pan upside down on a metallic rack where the bread will cool off before slicing it.

Nutrition: Calories 56.5; Fat 1.5 g; Carbs 10.1 g; Protein 2.3g

Made in the USA
Coppell, TX
25 November 2022

87017907R10037